CAMBRIDGE
UNIVERSITY PRESS

CAMBRIDGE
Global English

for Cambridge Primary English as a Second Language

Workbook 2

Elly Schottman, Paul Drury & Caroline Linse

Series Editor: Kathryn Harper

Shaftesbury Road, Cambridge CB2 8EA, United Kingdom

One Liberty Plaza, 20th Floor, New York, NY 10006, USA

477 Williamstown Road, Port Melbourne, VIC 3207, Australia

314–321, 3rd Floor, Plot 3, Splendor Forum, Jasola District Centre, New Delhi – 110025, India

103 Penang Road, #05–06/07, Visioncrest Commercial, Singapore 238467

Cambridge University Press & Assessment is a department of the University of Cambridge.

We share the University's mission to contribute to society through the pursuit of education, learning and research at the highest international levels of excellence.

www.cambridge.org
Information on this title: www.cambridge.org/9781108963657

First published 2014
Second edition published 2021

20 19 18 17 16 15 14 13 12 11 10

Printed in the Netherlands by Wilco BV

A catalogue record for this publication is available from the British Library

ISBN 978-1-108-96365-7 Workbook with Digital Access (1 Year)

Additional resources for this publication at www.cambridge.org/9781108963657

Cambridge University Press & Assessment has no responsibility for the persistence or accuracy of URLs for external or third-party internet websites referred to in this publication, and does not guarantee that any content on such websites is, or will remain, accurate or appropriate. Information regarding prices, travel timetables, and other factual information given in this work is correct at the time of first printing but Cambridge University Press & Assessment does not guarantee the accuracy of such information thereafter.

....

Contents

How to use this book

This workbook provides questions for you to practise what you have learned in class. There is a unit to match each unit in your Learner's Book.

Colour the stars at the beginning of each unit as you learn to do each thing.

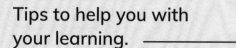

Colour in the stars as you learn to do each thing.

1 I can talk about classroom objects and school activities.
2 I can talk about the time and days of the week.
3 I can talk about parts of a book.
4 I can talk about who things belong to.
5 I can read and write words with short vowel sounds.
6 I can read and write about schools.

Tips to help you with your learning.

Language tip

all | most | some

Words to help you with your writing.

2 **Write the missing words.**
Use words from the box.

| came | very | said | must |
| first | was | new | |

There ¹_____ a contest in the forest.

All the animals ²_____.

The king Leopard ³_____, 'Thank you for coming.

You ⁴_____ throw this spear and quickly count to ten.

You must say "ten" before the spear hits the ground.

Each **Use of English** session is divided into three different levels. You can choose the level that is right for you.

Focus: these grammar questions help you to master the basics.

Focus

1 *next to, between, on, under*

All these people work in the community.
Can you say where each of them are standing?

| between | next to | under | on |

window cleaner

police officer

reporter

nurse

bus driver

farmer

painter

photographer

firefighter

street cleaner

- The bus driver is _____ the nurse.
- The reporter is _____ the police officer and the nurse.
- The paint pot is _____ the painter's chair.
- The cat is _____ the farmer's shoulder.
- The firefighter is _____ the photographer and the street cleaner.

Complete the sentence. Use the words **next to**, **between**, **under**, or **on**.

I am sitting _____.

Practice: these grammar questions help you to become more confident in using what you have learned.

Practice

2 **Write these questions in the correct word order.**

a have does many How a spider legs?

_____

b insects smell do How?

_____

c do What eat crickets?

_____

Challenge: these questions will make you think very hard.

Challenge

Would your own bug make a good indoor or outdoor pet? Why?

_____

_____

_____

Acknowledgements

The authors and publishers acknowledge the following sources of copyright material and are grateful for the permissions granted. While every effort has been made, it has not always been possible to identify the sources of all the material used, or to trace all copyright holders. If any omissions are brought to our notice, we will be happy to include the appropriate acknowledgements on reprinting.

Thanks to the following for permission to reproduce images:

Cover by Pablo Gallego (Beehive Illustration)

Inside Unit 1 pijama61/GI Stuart Fox/GI; BJI/GI; Unit 2 Art-Y/GI; Unit 3 Ariel Skelly/GI; redmal/GI; Wealan Pollard/GI; Pim Leojen/GI; Javier Fernández Sánchez/GI; Unit 5 Sezeryadigar/GI; Image Source/GI; neftali/Shutterstock; happytotakephoto/Shutterstock; Unit 6 arlindo71/GI; Lisbeth Hjort/GI; ryasick/GI; VStockLLC/GI; Borchee/GI; Africa Studio/Shutterstock; Halfpoint Images/GI; Unit 7 Andresr/GI; Unit 8 S. Greg Panosian/GI; Mohd Firdaus Haron/GI; Howard Koons/GI; Jose Luis Pelaez Inc/GI

GI = Getty Images

1 A day at school

Colour in the stars as you learn to do each thing.

1 ☆ I can talk about classroom objects and school activities.

2 ☆ I can talk about the time and days of the week.

3 ☆ I can talk about parts of a book.

4 ☆ I can talk about who things belong to.

5 ☆ I can read and write words with short vowel sounds.

6 ☆ I can read and write about schools.

1st place Shin
2nd place Nadia
3rd place Abeo

OUR STUDENTS AROUND THE W

I come from Nigeria

My classroom
My teacher
4+4=
My School

School Open Day 11am

Friday Family Fun 7 pm

Thursday Family Film Night

〉 1.1 Words around us

1 Write and colour.

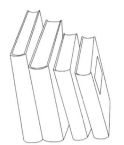

Colour two books blue.

Colour the map green.

Colour the calendar yellow.

Colour three clocks orange.

Colour the tablet red.

2 Which days do you go to school?

Circle the days you go to school.

Cross out the days you do **not** go to school.

Monday   Tuesday   Wednesday   Thursday

Friday   Saturday   Sunday

Challenge

What is your favourite day of the week? _____

〉 1.2 Our busy classroom

1 What time is it?

Look at each clock. Draw the missing clock hand to show the time.

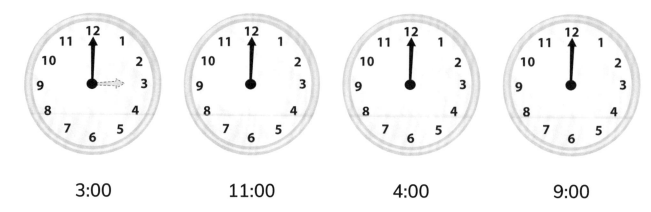

3:00   11:00   4:00   9:00

2 What do you do every day at school?

Read each question. Tick (✔) **yes** or **no**.

		yes	no
Do you do maths every day?			
Do you sing every day?			
Do you do writing every day?			
Do you have break time every day?			

Challenge

What language do you speak in your maths class? _____

3 Draw and write: A book for me!

Draw the cover of a book you would like to read.

Write the name of the book on the cover.

4 Write about your book.

What is the book about? Does your book tell a story or give real information?

_____

_____

_____

_____

5 Check your writing.

Use these writing tips:

☐ The first word of a sentence begins with a capital letter. **T**his is a book.

☐ A name begins with a capital letter. **A**my.

☐ Most sentences end with a full stop. My book is about a lion.

﹥ 1.3 Inside a book

1 Look at the book covers.

Draw a (circle) around each title.

Draw a line under the name of each author.

2 Choose a book.

Which of these books would you want to read?

_____

3 Look at the contents page.

Which book does it come from?

_____

How many chapters are in this book?

_____

Which chapter looks the most interesting?

CONTENTS

Where do snakes live?..........2

What do snakes eat?............8

Baby snakes......................12

Are snakes dangerous?......16

_____

4 Read and compare.

a In South Africa, Sizani and Nandi wear uniforms in their school.
Do you wear uniforms in your school?

_____

What are you wearing now?

Draw a picture and label your uniform.

b In China, Li Wei and his friends use paint in their art class.

Do you have art class in your school?

_____

What do you use to make art? Circle your answers.

Draw a line under the art materials you like best.

crayons   markers   paint   clay

Challenge

Find a book in your classroom with a contents page.

Title: _____

Author: _____

How many chapters are in the book? _____

> 1.4 Talking about possessions

Focus

1 Which box belongs to each person?

Draw lines to match.

Jill   Nick   Lucy

Jill's box   Nick's box   Lucy's box

Look at the pictures. Then fill the gaps.

___This___ box is ___mine___ .

___That___ box is _____ .

2 Answer the questions.

Whose box is this?

a   It's _____.

b   It's _____.

c   Which one is Lucy's box?

The _____ with _____.

Practice

3 Play a game.

Point to the things on your desk
and make sentences.

This is Aida's book.

This book is mine.

4 What is missing?

Trace the objects then complete the phrases.

a   <u>Oscar's</u> skipping rope

b   _____ lunchbox

c   Leo's _____

d   Ivy's _____ and _____

e   _____ jumper

Challenge ⭐

5 Sort out your pencil cases.

Mix the things in your pencil cases together. Say what belongs to whom.

The pencil sharpener is yours.

The red pencil is mine.

> 1.5 Review of short vowels

1 Find the vowels.

Circle the letters that are vowels.

a   H   T   I   r   O   b
   A   E   s   G   U
L   j   g   e   r

2 *sh, ch, th*

These letter combinations make a special sound.

shell   **ch**eese   **th**umb

Write the missing letters in the words below.

fi __ __   __ __ i r t y   __ __ i l d r e n

3 Just one letter is different.

These pairs of words are very similar! Just the vowel is different.
Write the correct vowel in each word.

s h __ p   s h __ p   p __ n   p __ n   b __ g   b __ g

4 **What is it?**

Write what each thing is. Use **a** or **an**.

ant

fish

octopus

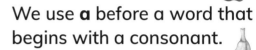

Language tip

We use **an** before a word that begins with a vowel.

It's **an a**pple.

We use **a** before a word that begins with a consonant.

It's **a** banana.

a  It's _____.

b  _____.

c  _____.

5 **Read and draw.**

Draw a big black bug in the box. Colour the box pink.
Draw a red hen next to the box.

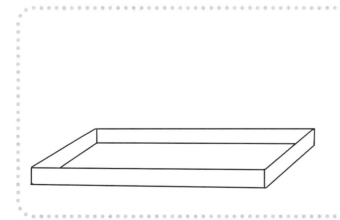

> 1.6 *My school*

1 **Look at the story about Fernando's school on pages 24 and 25 of your Learner's Book. Answer the questions about your school.**

The name of Fernando's school is Oceanside Primary School.

What is the name of your school? _____

Fernando's teacher is Ms Cruz.

What is your teacher's name? _____

In Fernando's classroom, there are tables and chairs.

There is a map and a calendar on the wall. What is in your classroom?

_____

_____

In science class, Fernando is learning about electricity.

What are you learning about in science?

_____

Fernando goes outside for break time.

Where do you go for break time?

_____

Fernando goes home from school at 2:00.

When do you go home from school? _____

2 Look at the pictures and write the words.

Use the box to help you.

maths	pool	paint	marker	science	read	play

m   a   r   k   e   r
   1

___ ___ ___ ___
    2

___ ___
  3   4

___ ___ ___ ___ ___
   5   6

___ ___ ___ ___ ___ ___ ___
  7   8

___ ___ ___ ___ ___
     9

___ ___ ___ ___
  10   11   12

Look for the numbers above. Each number has a letter above it.

Find each number, and write the letter above it on the lines below.
Then read the mystery sentence!

1		2	3	4		5	6		7	8	9	10	11	12

a   ___   ___ ___ ___   ___ ___   ___ ___ ___ ___ ___ ___

> 1.7 Check your progress

Listen to your teacher. Tick (✔) the correct pictures.

1 Find Shu Ling's pencil case.

 a ☐

 b ☐

 c ☐

2 What time is it?

 a ☐

 b ☐

 c ☐

3 What is Tom doing?

 a ☐

 b ☐

 c ☐

4 Which are John's?

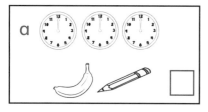 a ☐

 b ☐

 c ☐

Listen and write.

Listen and write. Then tick (✔) the picture of the word.

5 _____

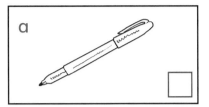

6 _____

7 Read and colour.

His book is red. His hat is black.

Reflection

Talk with a partner.

What are you good at?

☐ listening to and understanding English   ☐ reading in English

☐ talking in English   ☐ writing in English

☐ singing in English

What was your favourite activity?

_____

Why was it your favourite activity?

_____

2 Good neighbours

Colour in the stars as you learn to do each thing.

1 I can talk about workers in my neighbourhood.

2 I can learn about different jobs.

3 I can talk about where I live.

4 I can ask for and give directions.

5 I can read and write words with **-ar**, **-er**, **-ir**, **-or** and **-ur**.

6 I can read and talk about a poem and a song.

❯ 2.1 People in your neighbourhood

1 Write the missing words.

| window cleaner | police officer | reporter | nurse | bus driver |

The _____ is driving the bus.

The _____ is helping the boy.

The _____ is talking to the footballer.

The _____ is helping the lady cross the road.

The _____ is cleaning the window.

2 How many?

Look at the picture again. How many people can you see?

a How many children? _____

b How many grown-ups? _____

c How many people all together? _____

〉 2.2 Jobs

1   What is your job?

Look at each worker. Write the job that each person does.

| firefighter   nurse   window cleaner   police officer   bus driver   reporter |

a
Mrs Li is a

_____nurse_____.

d
Mr Stranova is a

_____.

b
Mrs Morelos is a

_____.

e
Richard Hermeis is a

_____.

c
Mr Rahman is a

_____.

f
Tanya McGee is a

_____.

2   Which item belongs to which person?

Draw lines to match.

3 Interview a member of your family.

Imagine you are a reporter. Interview a member of your family.

Choose 3 or 4 questions to ask.

What is your family member's name? _____

What is your job? _____

Where do you work? _____

How long have you worked at your job? _____

What is the hardest part of your job? _____

_____

What is the best part of your job? _____

_____

_____

Write the answers down as you interview your family member.

Then turn each answer into a sentence. For example, *My dad is a firefighter.*

Draw a picture of your family member beside your report.

4 Check your interview report.

Use these writing tips:

☐ Use 'he' if you are writing about a man.
Use 'she' if you are writing about a woman.

☐ Use capital letters at the beginning of sentences.

☐ Use full stops at the end of sentences.

☐ Check your spellings are correct.

〉 2.3 Where do you live?

1 Where do you live?

Name: _____

House or apartment number: _____

Street: _____

City or town: _____

Country: _____

Continent: _____

Challenge

What is your postal code?
Write your postal code here.

_____

2 How about you?

Silvia lives in an apartment building with a lift.
How about you? Write **yes** or **no**.

a Do you live in an apartment building?

_____

b Is there a lift in your building? _____

c Do you like going in a lift? _____

3 A letter to Silvia

Write to Silvia. Answer these questions in your letter.

What is your name?   Where do you live?

How old are you?   Who do you like to play with?

Dear Silvia,

_____

_____

_____

_____

_____

_____

Draw a picture
of you here.

Your friend,

_____

Write your name here.

> 2.4 Saying where things are

Focus

1 *next to, between, on, under*

All these people work in the community.
Can you say where each of them are standing?

between	next to	under	on

window cleaner

police officer

reporter

nurse

bus driver

farmer

painter

photographer

firefighter

street cleaner

- The bus driver is _____ the nurse.
- The reporter is _____ the police officer and the nurse.
- The paint pot is _____ the painter's chair.
- The cat is _____ the farmer's shoulder.
- The firefighter is _____ the photographer and the street cleaner.

Complete the sentence. Use the words **next to**, **between**, **under**, or **on**.

I am sitting _____.

Practice

2 Create sentences to say where things are.

Use the words in the box.

> my ruler   my backpack
>
> my skipping rope   behind
>
> in front of me   my book   on   under

a _My skipping rope is in front of me._

b _____

c _____

d _____

Challenge

3 Draw and write about what is around you.

_____

is in front of me.

_____

is behind me.

_____

is next to me.

Draw what is behind you.

This is you.

Draw what is next to you.

Draw what is next to you.

Draw what is in front of you.

> 2.5 Vowels followed by *r*

1 Write the name of the job.

Then draw a line to the correct picture.

a I paint.

I am a _____.

b I sing.

I am a _____.

c I dance.

I am a _____.

d I drive a taxi.

I am a _____.

> **Language tip**
>
> The names of jobs often end in **-er**.
>
> I teach. I am a teach**er**.
>
> When a verb ends in **-e**, we add only **-r**.
>
> I dance. I am a danc**er**.

2 Which job would you like to do when you are older?

Write a sentence. Then draw a picture.

When I grow up, I would like to be a _____.

3 Complete the crossword puzzle.

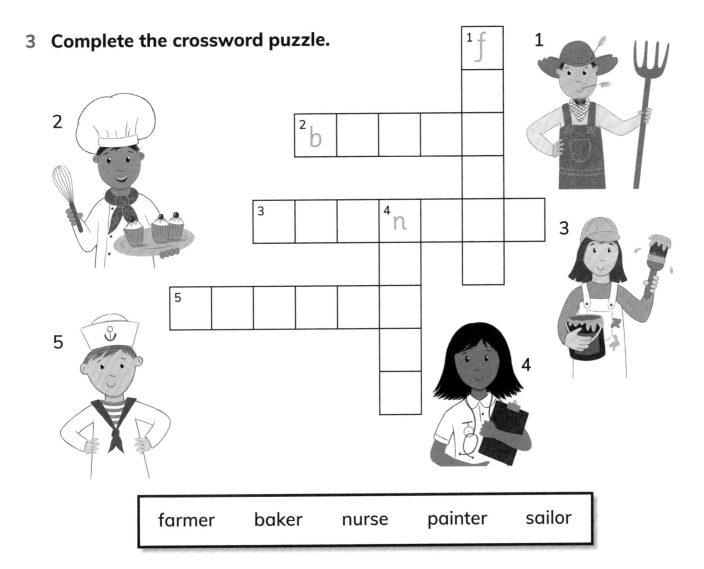

| | farmer | baker | nurse | painter | sailor |

Across →

2 I make bread. I am a...

3 I make pretty pictures I am a...

5 I work on boats I am a...

Down ↓

1 I grow and sell vegetables. I am a...

4 I help people who are sick. I am a...

> 2.6 A lot of kids

1 **Read the poem A Lot of Kids on page 40 of your Learner's Book again.**

Draw a picture based on the poem.

Write a sentence about your picture.
Check the Writer's checklist.

Writer's checklist

☐ Did you begin all names with a capital letter?

☐ Did you begin all sentences with a capital letter?

2 **Draw and write.**

Write a letter to an unknown friend.

Tell the friend your name, where you live and what you like to do.

Draw a picture to go with your letter.

Dear unknown friend,

My name is _____.

I live in _____.

I like to _____.

Your friend,

_____ (your name)

3 Draw and match.

Draw a line from each sentence to the matching picture.

Then colour the pictures.

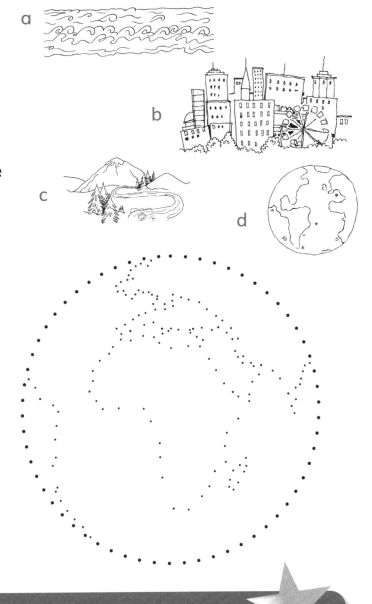

a

1 We've got **the rivers and the mountains** in our hands.

2 We've got **the seas and the oceans** in our hands.

b

3 We've got **the towns and the cities** in our hands.

c

4 We've got **the whole world** in our hands.

d

4 Connect the dots.

Circle the answer.
Then colour in the picture.

Is this our planet Earth?

Yes   No

Challenge

What can we do to make our planet a better place?

_____

_____

_____

〉 2.7 Check your progress

Listen to your teacher. Tick (✔) the correct pictures.

1 Which job are they talking about?

 a

 b

 c

2 Where is the cat?

 a

 b

 c

3 Find Lena's family.

 a

 b

 c

4 Where does Ramón live?

 a

 b

 c

5 Find Tony's dad.

 a

 b

 c

Listen and write.

6 What is Mrs Garcia's job?

She's an _____.

7 What is Mrs Wong's job?

She's a _____.

8 What is Mrs Demir's job?

She's a _____.

Write about you.

Read the question. Write your answer.

9 Where do you live?

_____

10 What's your favourite colour?

_____

Reflection

Talk with a partner.

What did you enjoy doing?

- [ ] interviewing my teacher
- [ ] writing a letter to Silvia
- [ ] completing the crossword puzzle

What would you like more help with?

- [ ] listening to and understanding English
- [ ] talking in English
- [ ] reading in English
- [ ] writing in English

3 ▶ Ready, steady, go!

Colour in the stars as you learn to do each thing.

☆1 I can talk about ways I can move.

☆2 I can read and talk about birds and what they can do.

☆3 I can talk about what people are doing.

☆4 I can read and write words with long vowel sounds.

☆5 I can read, talk and act out a play.

> 3.1 Different ways to move

1 Write the words on the lines.

| nose | foot | head | hand | tummy | fingers | toes | leg | arm |

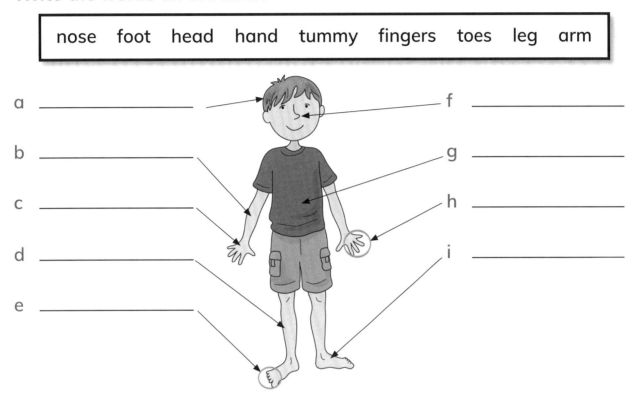

a _____

b _____

c _____

d _____

e _____

f _____

g _____

h _____

i _____

2 Draw a line to match the pictures with the words.

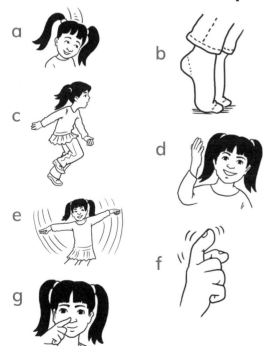

a

b

c

d

e

f

g

1 Touch your nose.

2 Wave your hand.

3 Wiggle your finger.

4 Hop on one foot.

5 Stand on your toes.

6 Flap your arms.

7 Nod your head.

> 3.2 Healthy and strong

1 Write it, read it, do it.

Write three sentences.

Use one word or phrase from each box.

Then read the sentences to your partner.

Clap		Tap		Nod	
Wave	your hands.	Hop on	one foot.	Shake	your head.
Shake		Stand on		Roll	

Wave your hands. _____

_____

_____

Do the actions with your partner.

2 Try this!

Can you do all three actions from your sentences at the same time?

(Circle) your answer.

Yes, I can.   No, I can't.

Can your partner do all three actions at the same time?

(Circle) your answer.

Yes, he can.   No, he can't.
Yes, she can.   No, she can't.

3 Choose and write.

Write about someone in your family.
Who are you going to write about?

_____

Name three activities and three healthy foods that they like.

Write the words in two columns in the table below.

Activities:

walking   running   dancing   biking   playing football   skipping rope

Food:

carrots   tomatoes   milk   apples   yogurt   oranges

_____ likes ...	
activities	food
1 _____	1 _____
2 _____	2 _____
3 _____	3 _____

Draw a picture of them doing something they like.

⟩ 3.3 What can birds do?

1 Draw a line to finish the sentences.

a **All** animals   can move.

b **All** animals   need water.

c **Most** birds   build nests.

d **Most** birds   can swim.

e **Some** birds   can fly

f **Some** birds   can't fly.

Language tip

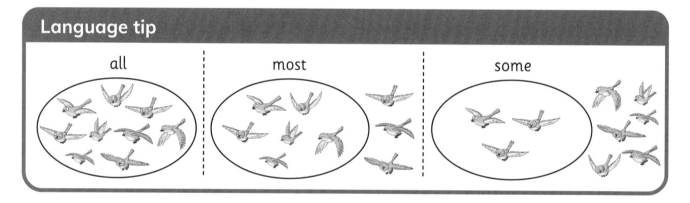

| all | most | some |

2 Which bird?

Look at the chart. Read the sentence and find the bird.

a This bird can walk, fly and climb trees, but it can't swim. _____

b This bird can walk and fly, but it can't swim or climb trees. _____

	swim	walk	fly	climb trees
penguin	✔	✔		
parrot		✔	✔	✔
crane		✔	✔	

Challenge

Write about a penguin. What can it do? What can't it do?

_____

_____

3 Draw a penguin.

Follow these steps.

1 Draw an egg shape without a top.

Draw a half circle on top.

Draw your penguin here.

2 Draw the penguin's beak.

Draw its tummy and its feet.

3 Draw the penguin's wings.

Draw a face.

〉 3.4 Describing ongoing actions

Focus

1 What are they doing?

Look at the picture and complete the sentences.

a (play) They are _____ playing _____ football.

b (kick) She is _____.

c (clap) He is _____.

d (eat) She _____.

e (skip) They _____.

What do you think? Circle the correct answer.

1 Do the parents like watching football?   **Yes, they do. / No, they don't.**

2 Do the children like playing football?   **Yes, they do. / No, they don't.**

Practice

2 Writing -ing words

Complete the sentences.

a They _____ are riding _____ bikes.

b We _____ ice cream.

c He _____ fruit.

ride

eat

buy

play

dance

d They _____ football.

e She _____.

f What are you doing? I _____.

3 What do you like doing?

Write down the things you *like doing* and ***don't like doing*** in your free time.

_____

_____

_____

_____

Challenge ⭐

4 What are you doing on holiday?

Now close your eyes and imagine you are on holiday.
Write what you are doing and draw a picture.

I am _____

_____

_____

❯ 3.5 Long vowel sounds

1 Words puzzle

Find and (circle) the words in the puzzle.

Some words go from left to right, like this: **W A V E**

Some words go from top to bottom, like this: **N I N E**

F	I	F	I	V	E	H	R	I	C	E
P	L	A	N	E	K	O	F	Q	A	N
R	R	O	P	E	I	M	I	P	K	I
C	W	A	V	E	T	E	R	J	E	N
B	W	R	I	T	E	X	E	P	F	E

wave

write

5 five

 rice

 rope

 plane

 home

9 nine

 cake

 kite

 fire

2 Long a spellings: a_e, -ai, -ay

Read and find words with the long **a** sound.

Write the words in a chart.
Write each word under the spelling that stands for the long **a** sound.

> On rainy days, the snails come out to play.
>
> We can sail away to a place on the bay.
>
> Take a train or a plane today.

Words with the long a sound		
a_e	ai	ay
place		

3 Look at the words in the chart.

Complete the sentences using words from the chart.

When it is _____, I need my umbrella.

We are going to _____ at the park _____.

I can see a _____ in the sky!

> 3.6 Bear and Turtle have a race

1 Find the turtles.

Find and colour each turtle.

How many turtles are there? _____

2 Did you know ...?

These animals are good swimmers!

Write the name of the two animals.

a _____.   b _____.

3 Running, jumping and swimming

Which animals can run, jump and swim? Finish the chart.

Draw a tick ✔ if you think the animal **can** do it.

Draw a cross ✗ if you think the animal **can't** do it.

	run	jump	swim
 turtle	✗	✗	✔
 bear			
 frog			
 deer			
 rabbit			

Challenge

Choose an animal. Write what it can do. Write what it can't do.

_____

_____

Draw a picture of the animal.

> 3.7 Check your progress

Listen to your teacher. Tick (✔) the correct pictures.

1 Find the correct picture.

 a
 b
 c

2 Find the correct bird.

 a
 b
 c

3 Which food does she not like?

 a
 b
 c

4 What does Lisa like doing?

 a
 b
 c

5 How is Bear feeling?

 a
 b
 c

Listen and write.

6 What is Lucy doing?

_____

_____

7 What is John doing?

_____

_____

Write and do.

8 Finish the sentence using the correct word from the brackets:

I saw a _____ *in the sky.* (plan / plane)

9 Write your name on the cake.

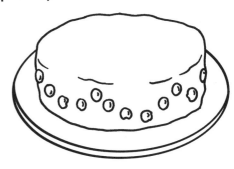

Write about you.

Read the question. Write your answer.

10 What do you like doing?

_____

_____

Reflection

Talk with a partner.

What do you enjoy learning about the most?

_____

Which activity would you like to do again, and why?

_____

4 The big sky

Colour in the stars as you learn to do each thing.

1. I can talk about shadows.
2. I can do experiments with shadows.
3. I can read and write about the Sun, Earth, Moon and stars.
4. I can read and talk about what people did in the past.
5. I can read and write words with long *i* sounds.
6. I can read and talk about a make-believe trip to the Moon.

The sky at night

〉 4.1 What do you know about shadows?

1 Label and colour.

Write the words on the labels.

| sun   shadows   sky   cloud |

Colour the Sun yellow.

Colour the shadows black.

Colour the sky blue.

Colour the cloud grey.

Challenge

Look at the sun in the picture. Look at the shadows.

What time of day is it? (Circle) the answer.

    morning   midday   evening

How can you tell?

〉 4.2 Light and shadow

1 Read and draw.

Look at these objects and then draw their shadows.

2 Look at the three sundials.

Which sundial do you like best? (Circle) your favourite and write a sentence.

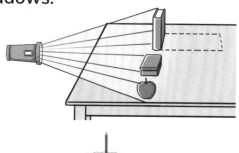

sundial A

sundial B

sundial C

I like sundial _____ best because _____.

Challenge

Can you use a sundial on a cloudy day? Why or why not?

_____

3 Make a sundial.

Put the instructions in the right order.

Write the numbers **1, 2, 3, 4** in the sun shapes.

 Push a pencil into the clay.

 Put a ball of clay on a paper plate.

 Mark the shadow in the morning and in the afternoon.

 Put your sundial in a sunny place.

4 Draw the shadow at midday.

You will need a small toy or object. Pretend your torch is the Sun.

Hold the torch above the toy, to show the Sun at midday.

Where is the shadow? Is the shadow long or short?

Draw the shadow on the diagram.

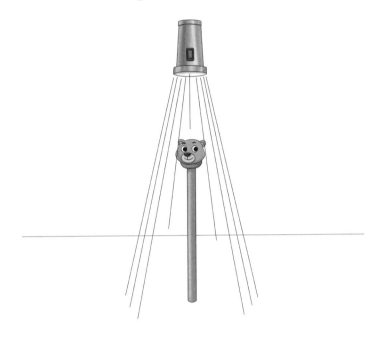

5 Draw the shadow in the evening.

Now hold the torch to show the Sun in the evening.

Where is the shadow now? Is the shadow long or short?

Draw the shadow on the diagram.

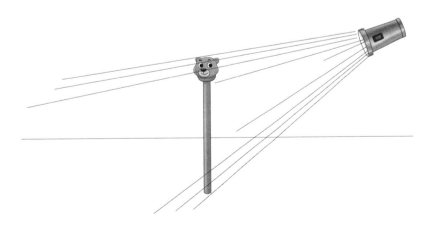

> 4.3 The Sun, Earth, Moon and stars

1 Read and write.

Label the Sun, Moon and Earth.

Circle the mistakes in each sentence. Then write the correct sentence.
The first one has been done for you.

a Seven planets circle around the Sun.

  Eight planets circle around the Sun.

b Earth is the fourth planet away from the Sun.

c The Moon is at the centre of the solar system.

d We can see the Sun in the night.

e The Sun gives us coolness and light.

f Without the Earth, there would be no life on the Sun.

2 Finish the picture.

It is night. Draw the Moon in the sky. The boy is holding a torch.
Draw the torch. The sky is dark. Colour the sky black.
The boy is shining the torch at the table.
Draw something on the table. What is it? _____

Then draw something under the table. What is it? _____

3 Draw and write.

Draw a picture of each item. Write a sentence for each pair of words.

Sun	Moon

Earth	stars

> 4.4 Using the past simple

Focus

1 Look at the picture and complete the sentences.

Use the words in the box.

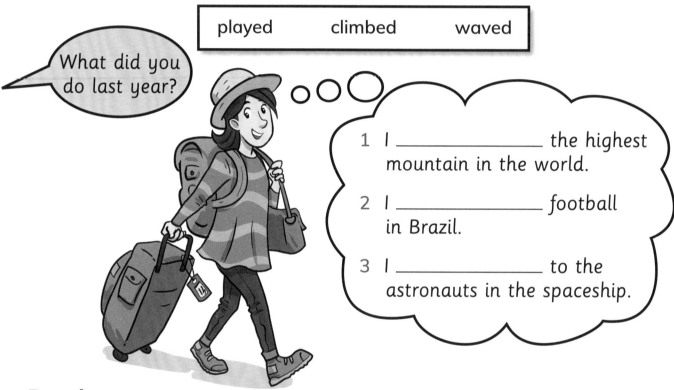

played   climbed   waved

What did you
do last year?

1 I _____ the highest mountain in the world.

2 I _____ football in Brazil.

3 I _____ to the astronauts in the spaceship.

Practice

2 What did you do?

Write **Yes**. Then answer the question.
Use verbs from the box.

climbed   played   waved

a Did you climb Mount Everest?

Yes. I climbed Mount Everest.

b Did you play football in Brazil?

_____

c Did you wave to the astronauts on the spaceship?

_____

Challenge

3 Write some questions, then ask a friend.

Write down their answers. Use words from the box.

wave / waved   go / went   travel / travelled   do / did   be / was / were
climb / climbed   walk / walked   watch / watched   talk / talked

a ___What did you do yesterday in the morning?___

_____

b What _____ _____ _____ yesterday, in the afternoon?

_____

c _____ _____ _____ _____ yesterday, in the evening?

_____

d _____ _____ _____ _____ yesterday, at night?

_____

4 What did you do yesterday?

a Who did you help?

_____

b How many people did you talk to?

_____

c What games did you play?

_____

> 4.5 Long *i*

1 Find the long *i* words.

Find and (circle) six words. They all make the long *i* sound.

Write the words next to the pictures.

d	f	b	i	t	e	g	r	l	i	g	h	t	e	i
f	s	h	i	n	e	l	i	n	i	g	h	t	q	w
w	r	i	t	e	v	c	m	n	m	k	i	t	e	t

 a _____

 b _____

 c _____

 d _____

 e _____

 f _____

2 How many long *i* words?

(Circle) the words with long *i* sounds.

(Five) white tigers are driving in a line at night.

How many can you find?

Write the number here. _____

3 Make some compound words.

Take one word from each half of the sun.
Put them together to make a longer word.

a _sun_ + _shine_ = _sunshine_

b _____ + _____ = _____

c _____ + _____ = _____

d _____ + _____ = _____

e _____ + _____ = _____

4 Read and draw.

Draw something that you
do **in the morning**.

Draw something that you
do **in the afternoon**.

Challenge

Name one thing that you do in the evening.

In the evening, I _____.

❯ 4.6 Our trip to the Moon

1 Write about the Moon and the Earth.

What do you know about the Moon? Use the words in the box to help you.

gravity	weigh less	jump high

1 _____

_____

2 _____

_____

3 _____

_____

What do you know about the Earth?

1 _____

_____

2 _____

_____

3 _____

_____

Challenge

The story on pages 74 to 76 in the Learner's Book is make-believe. Do you think it is possible to go into space on a field trip? Do you want to go on a field trip to the Moon? Why or why not?

_____

_____

2 Field trip report

Pretend you went on a field trip to the Moon.

What did you wear on the trip? Connect the dots to find out. Start from number 1.

What is it? Unscramble the word to find out.

e p a c s   t u i s

_____

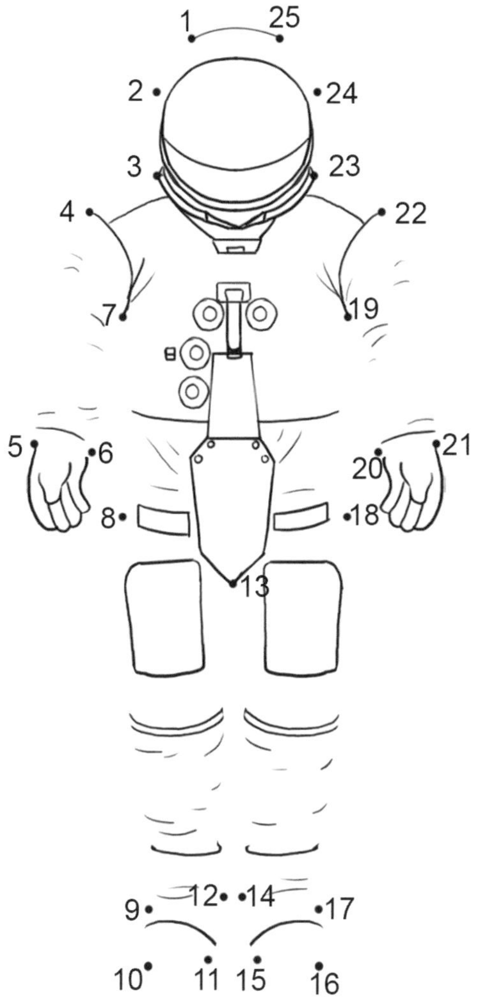

3 Answer questions about your field trip.

a What did you do on the trip?

_____

_____

b What did you see?

_____

_____

〉 4.7 Check your progress

Listen to your teacher. Tick (✔) the correct pictures.

1 The Moon circles the Earth, and the Earth circles the Sun.

 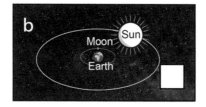 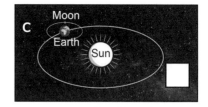

2 Find Mei's shadow.

3 Find the correct picture.

4 What did Tom do yesterday?

5 What did Lucy do yesterday?

Listen and write.

Listen and write the word. Then tick (✔) the correct picture.

6 _____

 a

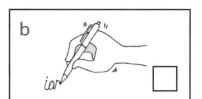 b

7 _____

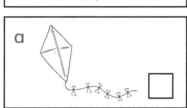 a

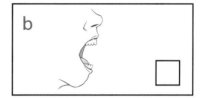 b

Read and write.

8 Read the sentence. Tick (✔) the correct picture.

The boy read a book about the sky.

 a

 b

Write about you.

9 Imagine a make-believe trip. Where did you go?

_____

10 What did you do?

_____

Reflection

Talk with a partner.

What do you do well?

☐ listening to and understanding English

☐ talking in English

☐ singing in English

☐ reading in English

☐ writing in English

What would you like to learn more about?

☐ the Sun

☐ the Earth

☐ the Moon

☐ the stars

5 Let's measure

Colour in the stars as you learn to do each thing.

1. I can count to 100.

2. I can name and describe shapes.

3. I can measure and say how long something is.

4. I can talk and write about what people did in the past.

5. I can read and write words that sound the same, like **one** / **won** and **two** / **too**.

6. I can read, discuss and act out a story.

❯ 5.1 Using numbers

1 Read and draw.

Read the instructions below.

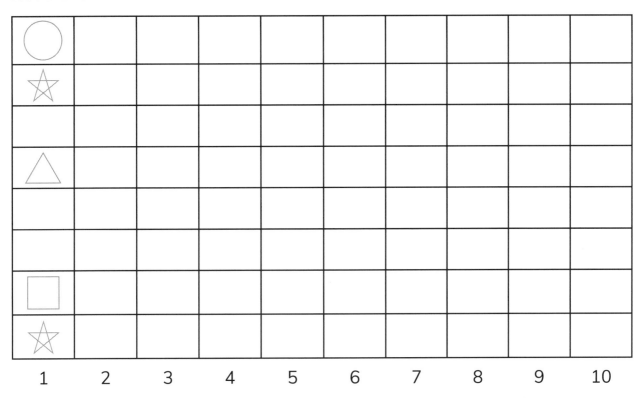

Start at the **bottom** of the chart.

- Draw 10 green stars.
- Draw 30 red squares.
- Draw 20 purple triangles.
- Draw 10 orange stars.
- Draw 10 blue circles.

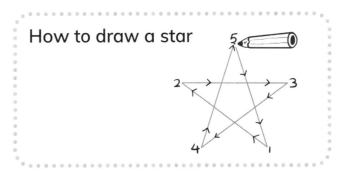

How to draw a star

How many stars are there altogether? _____

How many different shapes are there? _____

> 5.2 Shapes, patterns and numbers

1 Write the shapes.

Look at the clues. Then write the shape words in the crossword.

star

triangle

circle

heart

square

rectangle

Across →

2 ⭐

4 △

5 ⬤

Down ↓

1 ♥

2 ▢

3 ▢

Challenge

What is your favourite shape? _____

What is your favourite colour? _____

Draw your favourite shape. Use your favourite colour.

2 Read and follow the directions.

Colour all the big triangles green.

Colour all the squares yellow.

Colour all the hearts blue.

Colour all the small circles purple.

Colour all the big rectangles red.

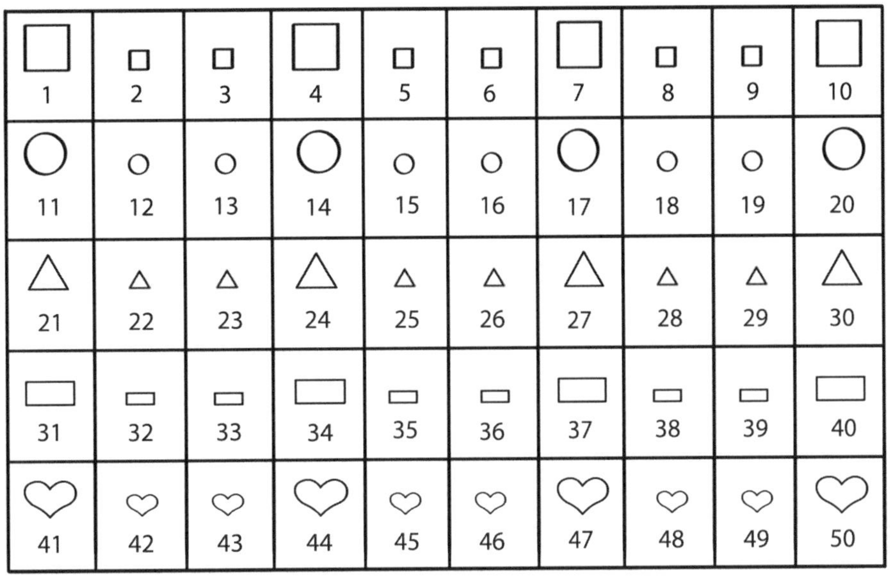

☐ 1	▫ 2	▫ 3	☐ 4	▫ 5	▫ 6	☐ 7	▫ 8	▫ 9	☐ 10
◯ 11	○ 12	○ 13	◯ 14	○ 15	○ 16	◯ 17	○ 18	○ 19	◯ 20
△ 21	△ 22	△ 23	△ 24	△ 25	△ 26	△ 27	△ 28	△ 29	△ 30
▭ 31	▭ 32	▭ 33	▭ 34	▭ 35	▭ 36	▭ 37	▭ 38	▭ 39	▭ 40
♡ 41	♡ 42	♡ 43	♡ 44	♡ 45	♡ 46	♡ 47	♡ 48	♡ 49	♡ 50

3 Look at the chart above.

Then answer the questions.

a What is the fifth shape?

Size: _____ Colour: _____ Shape: _____

b What is the tenth shape?

Size: _____ Colour: _____ Shape: _____

c What is the nineteenth shape?

Size: _____ Colour: _____ Shape: _____

d What is the twenty-fourth shape?

Size: _____ Colour: _____ Shape: _____

e What is the thirty-fourth shape?

Size: _____ Colour: _____ Shape: _____

f What shape is in the third row and third column? _____

〉 5.3 How did people measure long ago?

1   Measuring with your body

Use your fingers, hands and arms to measure – like the ancient
Egyptians did many years ago!

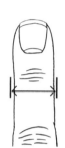   finger

   hand

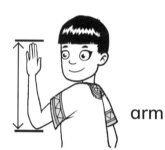   arm

a   How **high** is your chair?

_____ arms + _____ fingers

b   How **wide** is your chair?

_____ hands + _____ fingers

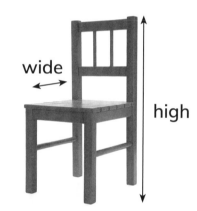

wide

high

c   How **long** is your pencil?

_____ hands + _____ fingers

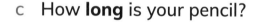

long

d   How **wide** is your book?

_____ hands + _____ fingers

wide

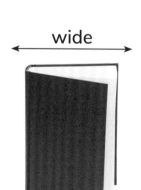

2 Measuring with a ruler

Use a centimetre ruler to measure the stamps.

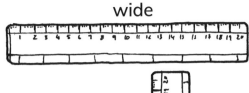

wide

a stamp from Mexico

a stamp from Thailand

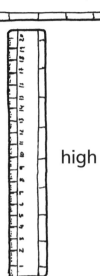

high

a   How **high** is the stamp from Mexico? _____ centimetres

b   How **wide** is the stamp from Mexico? _____ centimetres

c   How **high** is the stamp from Thailand? _____ centimetres

d   How **wide** is the stamp from Thailand? _____ centimetres

3 Estimate, then measure.

Estimate means **look and say what you think.**

cm means **centimetre.**

a   Estimate how **wide** the phone is.

I think the phone is about _____ cm wide.

b   Estimate how **high** the phone is.

I think the phone is about _____ cm high.

c   Now measure the phone.

The phone is _____ cm wide.

The phone is _____ cm high.

〉 5.4 Using the past simple (irregular verbs)

Focus

1 Find the past simple verb.

Read the verb. Then follow the line to find the past tense of each verb.

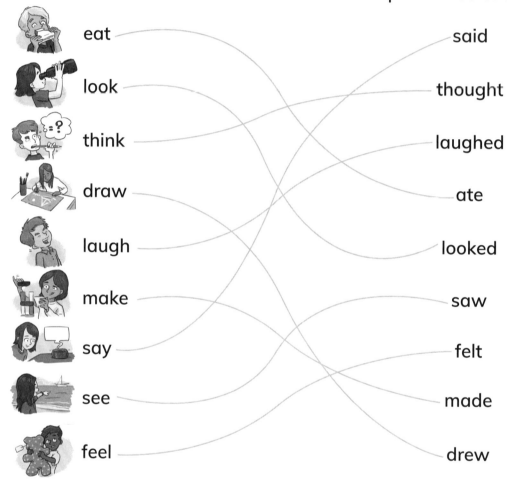

eat   said

look   thought

think   laughed

draw   ate

laugh   looked

make   saw

say   felt

see   made

feel   drew

Practice

2 Look at the picture and complete the questions and answers.

a What did the panda eat this morning?

It _____ bamboo.

b What _____ the panda _____ yesterday?

It ate bamboo.

Challenge

3 Choose the correct answer.

Think about the story about Birbal. (Circle) the correct answer.

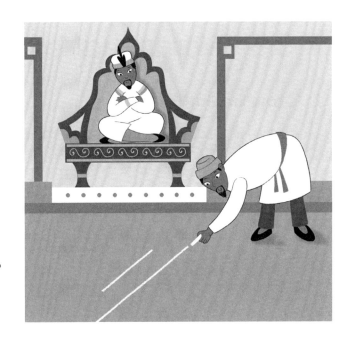

a What did Birbal draw?

He **drawed / drew / draws** a line.

b What did Birbal say to the king?

He **says / said**, 'My line is longer than your line.'

c What did the king **think / thinks / thought** about Birbal's answer?

He **thinks / thought** Birbal was very clever.

d Did the king feel cross?

No, he **feels / felt** happy. The king **laughs / laughed**.

4 Think about yesterday.

What did you eat yesterday? Write three things.

I ate _____.

What did you see yesterday? Write three things.

I _____.

Where did you go yesterday?

I _____.

〉 5.5 Words that sound the same

1 Draw and match.

Draw a (circle) around the number words.

Then draw a line between each pair of words that sound the same.

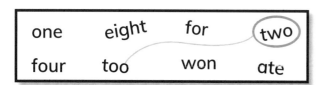

one	eight	for	(two)
four	too	won	ate

Language tip

In English, the number word comes before the size and colour word.

I won one little blue apple.

2 Write silly sentences.

Use the number words and words that sound the same as the number words.

_____

_____

_____

3 Write the correct words on the lines.

for   **four**

These _____ frogs are

_____ Annisa's friend.

too   **two**

Yusuf has two turtles, and Hamza

has _____ turtles _____.

What is missing from each drawing? Draw it!

Say each sentence three times quickly!

4 Read Finn's maths poem.

Then write how old each person is.

My family

Mary is five and Bea is three,
Billy is nine, that's three times Bea.
In four more years, I'll be eleven,
That's much better than being seven.
My grandpa's sixty, I'm told.
How many years till I'm that old?

Mary ___5___   Bea _____   Billy _____   Grandpa _____

Challenge

a Finn says, 'In four more years, I'll be eleven.'

How old is Finn now? _____

b Finn says, 'My grandpa's sixty, I'm told.
How many years till I'm that old?' Do the maths!

Answer the question. _____

---

5 Draw Finn's family.

Draw the people in the poem. Write their ages.

> 5.6 Many ways to count to ten

1 Which character?

King Leopard   Elephant   Water Ox   Chimpanzee   Little Antelope

Read the clues. Write the name of the character.

a   This animal has two horns. It was the **second** animal to throw the spear. _____

b   This animal can walk on two legs. It was the **third** animal to throw the spear. _____

c   This animal is big, heavy and grey. It was the **first** animal to throw the spear. _____

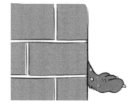

d   This animal is yellow with black spots. This animal said, 'It's time to choose a new king.' _____

e   This animal is small, quiet and clever. It won the contest and became the new king. _____

2 **Write the missing words.**
Use words from the box.

came	very	said	must
	first	was	new

There ¹_____ a contest in the forest.

All the animals ²_____.

The king Leopard ³_____, 'Thank you for coming.

You ⁴_____ throw this spear and quickly count to ten.

You must say "ten" before the spear hits the ground.

The winner of the contest will be the ⁵_____ king.'

The elephant was the ⁶_____ to try.

'I'm ⁷_____ big,' he said. 'I think I can do it.'

3 **Complete the counting patterns.**

Counting in twos is a counting pattern. Counting in tens is another counting pattern. Write the missing numbers in each pattern.

two   four   six   _____   _____   twelve

ten   twenty   _____   forty   _____

Challenge

These counting patterns are more difficult! Can you do them?

twelve   ten   eight   _____   _____   two

one hundred   ninety   eighty   _____   _____   fifty

〉 5.7 Check your progress

Listen to your teacher. Tick (✔) the correct pictures.

1 Find the correct chart.

 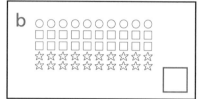 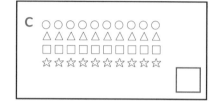

2 Find the correct number.

3 Find the correct animal.

4 What did Tony buy?

 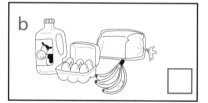 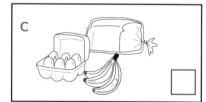

5 What did Sarah buy?

Listen and write.

6 How long is Jack's pencil? _____ cm

7 Is the elephant loud or quiet? _____

Read and write.
Finish each sentence using the correct word from the brackets.

8 This cake is _____ you. (four / for)

9 What time is it? It's _____ o'clock. (two / too)

Draw and write.

10 Draw an animal. What did you draw?

_____

Reflection

Talk with a partner.

What is your favourite activity?

_____

What did you enjoy most in this unit?

☐ learning numbers 10–100

☐ learning about words that sound the same

☐ singing a song about numbers

☐ reading a story about animals in the forest

What do you want more help with?

☐ learning numbers 10–100

☐ learning about words that sound the same

☐ singing a song about numbers

☐ reading a story about animals in the forest

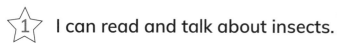

6 ▶ All about bugs

Colour in the stars as you learn to do each thing.

☆ 1   I can read and talk about insects.

☆ 2   I can learn about insects.

☆ 3   I can say how spiders and insects are similar and different.

☆ 4   I can write questions and answer them.

☆ 5   I can read and write words with the spelling **ee** and **ea**.

☆ 6   I can read, discuss and act out a story.

› 6.1 Bugs and other garden animals

1 Draw a line to match the animal to its description.

   a It has 4 colourful wings.   bee

   b It is yellow and black.   cricket

   c It makes a web.   spider

   d It lives in the ground.   ant

   e It has wings but can't fly.   worm

   f It is an insect that doesn't have wings.   butterfly

2 Write.

Look for some ants, a butterfly, some bees and a worm in the picture.

Then write about the picture. Use **above**, **behind**, or **between**.

For example: The spider is **above** the chair.

   a The butterfly is _____ the worm.

   b The ants are _____ the chair and the flowers.

   c The bee is _____ the flowers.

   d The tree is _____ the chair.

3 Draw two more bees in the picture. Draw a spider on the web.

> 6.2 Crickets and other insects

1 Learn about crickets.

Look at three **headings** in the text about crickets.

There is a sentence missing under each heading.

Find each missing sentence at the bottom of the page. Write it on the line.

Crickets

What does a cricket look like?

A cricket has six legs, two wings and two antennae.

_____

How do crickets move?

Crickets have wings, but most crickets do not fly.

_____

How do crickets communicate?

Crickets sing by rubbing their wings together. Crickets have different songs with different meanings.

_____

Other crickets understand their songs.

Crickets are different colours and sizes.

Crickets jump. Their back legs are very strong.

2 **Would it be good to have a pet cricket?**

Make a list of reasons why it would be good to have a pet cricket, and reasons why it would not be good.

Reasons to have a pet cricket	Reasons not to have a pet cricket
It makes me happy.	Crickets don't like the cold.

3 **Draw a cricket in the picture.**

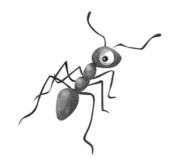

> 6.3 Ants and spiders

1 How are spiders and ants the same?

Circle the sentences that are true for both spiders **and** insects.

They have more than four legs.   They have more than four eyes.

They can climb.   They carry their food home.

They have antennae.   They make webs.

2 Complete the Venn diagram.

Write one fact from Activity 1 in each section of the Venn diagram.

Only true for ants

True for ants and spiders

Only true for spiders

Challenge

How are spiders and humans similar?

_____

How are spiders and humans different?

_____

3 Draw a picture of your very own bug.

Write about your bug.

What is your bug's name?

_____

What does it look like?

_____

Where does it live?

_____

What does it eat?

_____

Writer's checklist

☐ Begin each sentence with a capital letter.

☐ Put a full stop at the end of each sentence.

Challenge

Would your own bug make a good indoor or outdoor pet? Why?

_____

_____

_____

> 6.4 Writing questions

Focus

1 **Complete the questions.**

> How many... do   What do...
> Where do...

a **Bee:** _____ butterflies eat?

Butterfly: Pollen

Bee: Me too!

b **Bee:** _____ butterflies sleep?

Butterfly: In trees or shrubs.

Bee: Bees sleep in a beehive.

c **Bee:** _____ wings _____ butterflies have?

Butterfly: 4

Bee: Me too!

Practice

2 **Write these questions in the correct word order.**

a have does many How a spider legs?

_____

b insects smell do How?

_____

c do What eat crickets?

_____

Challenge

ladybird   dragonfly   caterpillar

3 **Choose one insect.**

Write questions and research the answers.

a How many legs does a ladybird have?

_____

b What does _____?

_____

c How does _____?

_____

d Where does _____?

_____

4 **Write questions to ask a friend.**

Use your imagination! One has been done for you.

a How many legs do spiders have?

b How _____?

c Do _____?

d What _____?

❯ 6.5 Rhyming words, words with long **e**

1 Complete the crossword puzzle.

Look at the clues. Write the words.

Across →

1    5

6 **3**   7

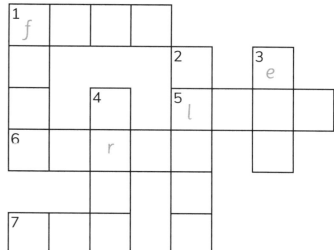

Down ↓

1    2    3    4

Challenge

Write some rhyming poems.
The words in the box will help you.

| bee | me | flea | tea | knee | tree |

1, 2, 3. I can see a _____.

1, 2, 3. There's a bug on _____.

1, 2, 3. There's a bug in the _____.

2 Make your own new silly version of the poem.

Make sure that the poem rhymes.

| knee | bread | flea | red | me | bed | bee | head | she | the sea |

A bee and a _____

had breakfast with _____.

The bee bumped his _____

and went back to _____.

Draw a picture for your poem.

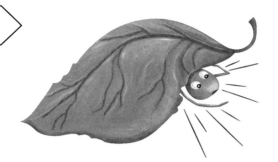

> 6.6 Little Ant

1 Little Ant's problem

Think about the story of Little Ant. Read the questions. Write your answers.

a What fell on Little Ant? _____

b Little Ant asked a mouse, a cat and a dog for help.

   Did they help Little Ant? _____

   Why or why not? _____

2 The solution

Cousin Flea helped Little Ant! Finish the sentences.

Write the past tense of the verb in brackets on the line.

a Cousin Flea _____ the dog. (bite)

b The dog _____ the cat. (scare)

c The cat _____ the mouse. (chase)

d The mouse _____ the leaf. (lift)

e Little Ant _____ home to her mother. (run)

3 What happened next?

Little Ant came home to her mother.
She and her mother were very happy.
What do you think they did after this?
What do you think they ate?
What did they say?
Draw a picture.

Challenge

Write sentences to go with your picture.

_____

_____

_____

❯ 6.7 Check your progress

Listen to your teacher. Tick (✔) the correct pictures.

1 Find the correct insect.

2 Where are the animals?

3 Which image is correct?

4 How does a bee hear sounds?

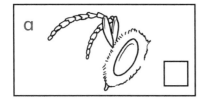 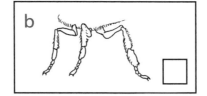 

5 Tick (✔) the correct image.

Listen and write.

6   How many eyes does this spider have? _____

7   What insect makes honey? _____

Read and write.

8   (Circle) the three words that rhyme with *me*.

    tea   the   she   tree

9   Is this a picture of an ant or a spider? _____

10 How do you know?

_____

_____

Reflection

Talk with a partner.

What is your favourite bug? _____

Which animal would you most like as a pet? _____

What was your favourite activity? _____

What would you like to improve?

☐ listening to and understanding English

☐ reading and writing words with long ee spelling

☐ comparing insects and spiders

☐ reading and talking about a story

☐ writing and answering questions

Colour in the stars as you learn to do each thing.

☆ **1** I can talk about caring for planet Earth.

☆ **2** I can learn about plants.

☆ **3** I can learn about trees and recycling.

☆ **4** I can role-play conversations at a market.

☆ **5** I can read and write words with long **o** spellings.

☆ **6** I can read and discuss a biography.

CARING FOR THE EARTH

Wangari Maathai

OWLS OF THE WORLD

> 7.1 Caring for planet Earth

1 Look at the picture and describe what the people are doing.

Write the name of the person next to each description.

I'm drawing the birds. _____

I'm picking up the rubbish. _____

I'm recycling. _____

We're planting trees. _____ _____

I'm watering the trees. _____

› 7.2 Plants and flowers

1 Read and answer the questions.

Tick (✔) **yes** or **no** for each question.

	yes	no
1 Do green leaves clean the air outside?		
2 Do green leaves clean the air inside?		
3 Do plants make the air dirty?		
4 Do plants need water?		
5 Do roots grow tall?		

2 Write the labels on the picture.

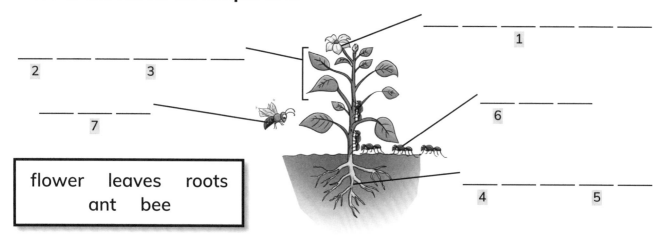

_____ _____ _____ _____ _____
1

_____ _____ _____   _____ _____ _____
2   3

_____ _____ _____
7

_____ _____ _____
6

_____ _____ _____ _____
4   5

flower   leaves   roots
ant   bee

3 Look at the picture above and look for the numbers.

Find each number, and write the letter above it on the lines below.
Then read the mystery sentence!

Mystery sentence

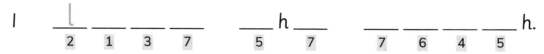

I ___ ___ ___ ___   ___ h ___   ___ ___ ___ ___ h.
   2   1   3   7   5   7   7   6   4   5

Challenge

Write three things you like about the Earth.

_____

_____

_____

4 Answer the questions.

a What plants and animals do you like best?

_____

b Describe the sky and the weather.

_____

c What can you see, hear, smell and feel outside?

_____

5 Write your own poem.

The Earth is my home.

I love _____

The sight of _____

The smell of _____

The sound of _____

I will take care of the Earth.

〉 7.3 The importance of trees

1 **Read, colour and draw.**

Draw a bird's nest on the tree. Draw two baby birds in the nest.

Draw some green leaves and some cherries on the tree.

Draw a mother bird flying in the sky. Colour the sky blue.

Draw green grass on the ground and three yellow flowers.

Draw a butterfly on a flower.

Draw some roots at the bottom of the tree.

2 Wood from trees

Trees give us wood. How do people use wood?

We use wood to make _____.

We use wood to make _____.

We use wood _____.

3 Food from trees

(Circle) four foods that come from trees.

apple

potatoes

bread

orange juice

pear

nuts

4 How can we save trees?

(Circle) three ideas that can help.

Recycle paper.

Write on both sides of the paper.

Make fires.

Plant new trees.

Cut down more trees.

Challenge

Write one new fact you learned about trees.

_____

› 7.4 Using **this** and **these**, **that** and **those**

Focus

1 **Look at the picture and complete the sentences.**

| stem | tomatoes | leaf | flowers |

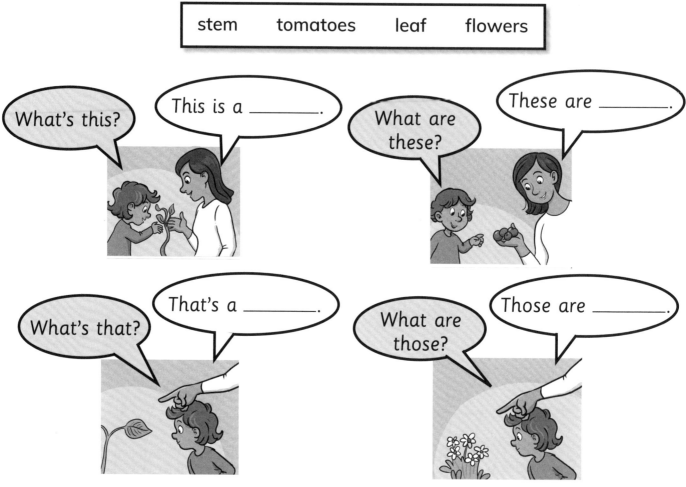

What's this?

This is a _____.

What are these?

These are _____.

What's that?

That's a _____.

What are those?

Those are _____.

Practice

2 **Complete the sentences.**

a What's this?

This is a _carrot_.

b What are those?

Those are _____.

Challenge

3 Complete the questions and answers.

a <u>What are these?</u>   _____ bananas.

b _____   This a pineapple.

c What are _____?   _____ oranges.

d _____   _____ a watermelon.

4 Play a game with a partner. Guess the sound.

› 7.5 Long o

1 Mystery picture

Read each word in a shape.

If the word has the **long o** sound, colour the shape **blue**.

If the word has the **short o** sound, colour the shape **green**.

If the word has the *ow* sound in **how**, colour the shape **brown**.

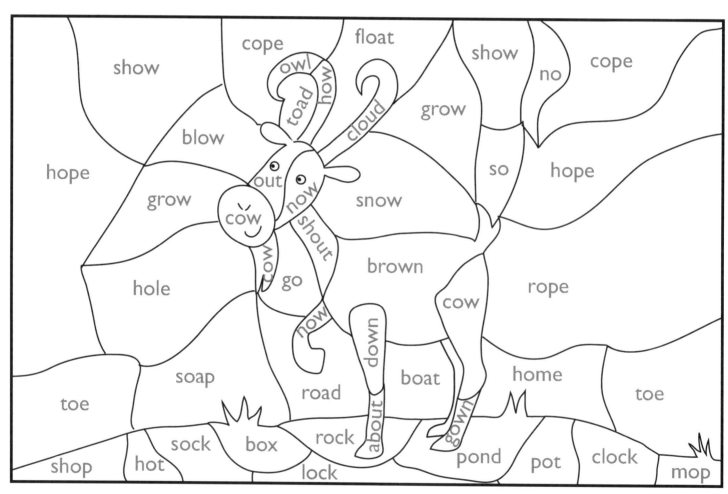

The mystery picture is a brown _____.

2 Find the long o sounds.

Read the story. (Circle) all the words with the long o sound.

The clever crow

An (old) (crow) is looking for water to drink.

He sees a hole in the ground.

At the bottom of the hole, there is some water!

The crow can't reach the water.

The crow thinks and thinks.

'I know what to do!' he says.

There are lots of little stones on the ground.

The crow throws a stone in the hole.

He throws lots of stones in the hole.

Slowly, the hole fills with stones.

The water in the hole gets

higher and higher.

Finally, the crow can reach the water.

He drinks and drinks.

Challenge

Make a sentence with these words.

crow   The   very   clever   old   was

_____

> 7.6 Wangari Maathai

1 Find the countries.

Wangari was born in **Kenya**.
She went to school in the
United States and then
Germany. Then she came
back to Kenya.

Find these countries on a
map or globe. Write the
names on this map.

Draw arrows to show the
route Wangari travelled.

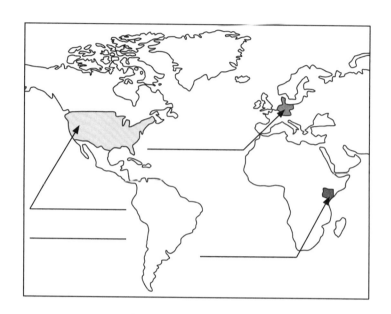

2 Unscramble the words.

Put the letters in the correct order. Write the numbers on the picture.

1 r e e t   t __ __ __

2 o i l s   s __ __ __

3 e l h o   h __ __ __

4 r e t a w   w __ __ __ __

3 Write your own autobiography.

An autobiography is the story of your life.

Write your autobiography. Answer the questions.

a Where were you born?

I was born in _____.

b Write two interesting things that have happened to you. How old were you?

When I was _____, _____

               (age)

_____.

When I was _____, _____

               (age)

_____.

c What would you like to do when you grow up?

When I grow up, I would like to _____

_____.

d Draw a picture of how you will look when you are grown up!

105 ⟩

〉 7.7 Check your progress

Listen to your teacher. Tick (✔) the correct pictures.

1 Who is helping to take care of the earth?

2 Which sign is being described?

3 Which plant is being described?

4 Find the correct picture.

5 Find the correct picture.

Listen and write.

6 Which part of a tree helps clean the air?

_____

7 Which part of a tree grows under the ground?

_____

8 (Circle) the four words that have the long **o** sound.

   hole   hop   pot   go   road   rock   crow

Read and write.

9 What is this girl doing to help save trees?

_____

10 What are these boys doing to help save trees?

_____

Reflection

Talk with a partner

What did you do well in this unit?	What would you like more help with?
☐ reading, talking and writing about caring for the Earth	☐ reading, talking and writing about caring for the Earth
☐ learning about trees and other plants	☐ learning about trees and other plants
☐ learning about recycling	☐ learning about recycling
☐ role-playing a conversation in the market	☐ role-playing a conversation in the market
☐ reading and discussing a biography	☐ reading and discussing a biography

Colour in the stars as you learn to do each thing.

1 I can talk and write about different kinds of homes.

2 I can talk about things I do at home.

3 I can read about different kinds of homes.

4 I can talk about things in the future, using **will**.

5 I can read and write words with long **u** spellings.

6 I can read and discuss informational text.

> 8.1 Different kinds of homes

1 Write and draw.

Answer the questions.

Look at the Picture Dictionary on page 173 of the Learner's Book for ideas.

a Can you think of an animal that lives in trees? _____

_____

b Can you think of an animal that lives in a hole? _____

_____

c Can you think of an animal that lives in a shell? _____

_____

d Can you think of an animal that lives near water? _____

_____

2 Write your own version of the poem.

Look at the poem in the Learner's Book on page 131. Work with a partner.

Your poem can be about homes for animals or homes for people!

〉 8.2 Inside a home

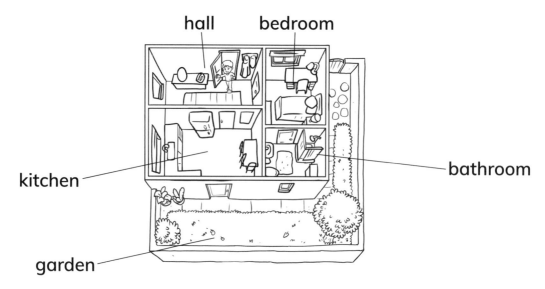

1 Where do you do these things?

a Where do you play?

_____

b Where do you brush your teeth?

_____

c Where do you dress?

_____

d Where do you eat your breakfast?

_____

2 Join the dots.

Draw lines to join the dots 1–30. Then colour the house.

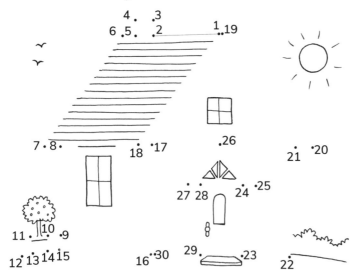

Write these words next to the things:

roof   wall   door   window

3 **Tick (✔) yes or no.**

Do you help out at home?

Put a tick (✔) to show which things you **do** or **don't do.**

Ways to help out at home	yes	no	Ways to help out at home	yes	no
set the table			put dishes in the sink		
tidy my room			put my clothes away		
make my bed			sweep the floor		

Challenge

What is your favourite way to help at home?

_____

4 **Read the following riddles.**

Answer the questions using words from the box.

table	lamp
chair	shower
refrigerator	sink

a You sit on me. What am I? _____

b I light up the room. What am I? _____

c I keep food cold. What am I? _____

d You sit around me. You put your food on me. What am I? _____

5 **Write your own riddles.**

Think of some things you might have in a house.

Write your own riddles for these things.

_____

_____

❯ 8.3 Homes around the world

1 **Where can you find these homes?**

Read the country name under each photo.
Then find the country on a map. Answer the questions.

Adobe house in Ghana

Stilt house in Borneo

Cave house in Turkey

Which country is furthest from where you live? _____

Which country is nearest to where you live? _____

2 **Which one?**

Write the answer on the line: **adobe house, stilt house** or **cave house**.

a Which home is built above water? _____

b Which home is made of mud? _____

c Which home is made of rock? _____

Challenge

Which home is the strongest? _____

Why? _____

3 Read and draw the best house for each person.

I live somewhere very hot in the summer and very cold in the winter.

This house is a cave house in Turkey .

I live somewhere very dry.

This house is _____.

I live in a big city.

This house is _____.

I live somewhere where there is water everywhere.

This house is _____.

> 8.4 Using future form *will*

Focus

1 Match the characters to their dream homes.
Finish the sentences.

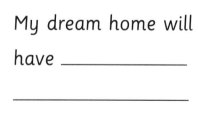

My dream home will
have _____
_____
_____.

My dream home will
have _____
_____
_____.

My dream home will
have _____
_____
_____.

Practice

2 **Read and (circle) the correct one.**

What will the playground have?

It ¹**has / will have** two slides. One ²**is / will be** very curvy, the other one ³**will have / will be** very high. The playground ⁴**does / will have** a rope ladder and a bridge. Oh, and it ⁵**has / will have** lots of swings so lots of children can swing at the same time.

3 **Look at the picture and complete the sentences.**

Now I have three seeds. In a few weeks,

I will have _three plants_.

Now I have four eggs. In a few months,

I will have _____.

Now I have a messy room. In a few minutes,

I _____.

Challenge

4 **Draw a picture and write about your dream home.**

| slide | ladder | swimming pool | zoo | balloon | spaceship | lift |

My dream home will have

_____

_____

_____

_____

〉 8.5 Long **u** and **oo**

1 Crossword puzzle

Look at the clues. Write the words.

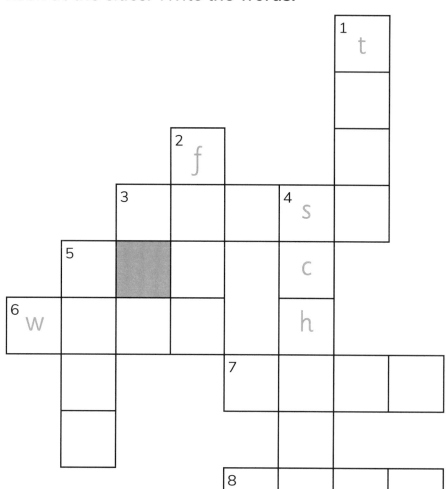

Across →

3

6

7

8

Down ↓

1

2

4

5

Challenge

Most of the words have the sound like in **shoe**.

Two words have a short sound like in **look**. Write the words.

_____ _____

2 Words with the long u and oo sound

Draw a <u>line</u> under each word that has the
long **u** and **oo** sound.

(Circle) the letters that make the long **u** sound.

The huge blue goose flew to the moon.

3 My favourite room

What is your favourite room in your home? _____.

Draw a picture of the room. Draw things in the room.
Write the words next to the things you draw.

Look at page 168 of the Picture Dictionary in the Learner's Book.
You will find some words to help you.

› 8.6 Where do animals build homes?

1 Comparing animal homes

Read the text on pages 140 to 142 in the Learner's Book to find the answers.

Write **B** (beaver), **R** (rabbit) or **T** (termite).

a Whose home is under the ground? ☐

b Whose home is under and above the ground? ☐

c Whose home is in a pond? ☐

d Whose home has special rooms for babies or eggs? ☐ ☐

e Whose home is made with branches? ☐

f Whose home is made just of mud? ☐

2 Animal enemies

'When a rabbit sees a fox or other **enemy***, it stamps on the ground with its back foot.'*

1 What does the word **enemy** mean in this sentence?

Tick (✔) the correct answer.

a an animal with a long tail ☐

b an animal that eats rabbits ☐

c an animal that lives above ground ☐

2 Name an animal that is an enemy of a beaver. _____

3 Name an animal that is an enemy of a mouse. _____

3 Picture quiz

Look at pages 140 to 142 of the Learner's Book.

a How many rabbits (babies and grown-ups) can you see

in the picture of the rabbit home? _____

b How many underwater doors can you see in the picture

of the beaver home? _____

c Which animal home looks most like a beehive house? _____

4 A rabbit poem

A **bunny** is another word for a rabbit.

When a bunny **pricks up its ears**, that means it puts its ears straight up.

Write the missing words in this poem. Use words from the box.

ground	bunny	hole	jumps	sound

Here is a ¹_____ with ears so funny.
And here is its ²_____ in the ground.
When a ³_____ it hears, it pricks up its ears.
And ⁴_____ in its hole in the ⁵_____.

❭ 8.7 Check your progress

Listen to your teacher. Tick (✔) the correct pictures.

1 Which room is being described?

2 Which is Jill's tree house?

  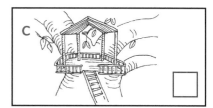

3 What do you need to do?

 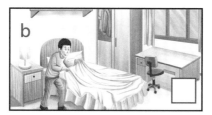 

4 Where does Ahmed live?

5 Where will Nina live?

Listen and write.

6 Listen to the clues. Put the letters in the right order to make the name of the animal.   b i b r t a _____

Read and write.

Put the letters in the right order to make the word.

7 f o o r _____

8 t b u e s _____

9 m n o o _____

10 What would you like in your playground? Choose two things. Complete the sentences.

slide   ladder   swing   seesaw

I'd like a _____.

I'd _____ too.

Reflection

Talk with a partner.

What are you good at?

☐ talking and writing about different kinds of homes

☐ talking about rooms and furniture in a home

☐ talking about things we do at home

☐ reading about different kinds of home

What would you like more help with?

☐ listening to and understanding English

☐ talking in English

121

9 ▶ Let's explore the city!

Colour in the stars as you learn to do each thing.

⭐1 I can talk about city things and places.

⭐2 I can use describing words.

⭐3 I can follow and give directions.

⭐4 I can talk and write about the past, present and future.

⭐5 I can use opposite words.

⭐6 I can read and discuss a story.

❯ 9.1 Things in a city

1 Follow and write.

Where are Malik and his friends going?

Follow the lines to find out. Then complete the sentences using phrases below.

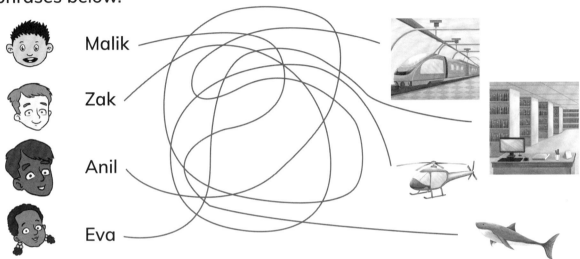

likes riding in a helicopter	likes visiting the library
likes looking at the sharks	likes riding the underground

Malik _____ _____.

Zak _____ _____.

Anil _____ _____.

Eva _____ _____.

2 So do I!

Do you like the same things as Malik?

If you like it, write **So do I**!

If you don't like it, write **I don't**!

Malik: I like ice cream!

You: _____

Malik: I like watching TV!

You: _____

Malik: I like singing!

You: _____

> 9.2 At the aquarium

1 Word search puzzle

Colour the animal picture clues.

Do the word search.

J	S	E	A	H	O	R	S	E	A
N	E	A	S	H	A	R	K	S	T
F	E	L	D	O	D	U	E	E	L
U	J	E	L	L	Y	F	I	S	H
D	B	T	U	R	T	L	E	L	M
M	B	O	C	T	O	P	U	S	A
E	M	V	R	J	F	I	O	M	T
P	E	N	G	U	I	N	S	W	O
U	L	U	Y	U	G	C	J	H	E
A	L	L	I	G	A	T	O	R	I

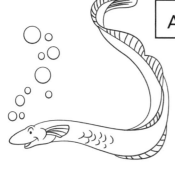

2   Write about a mystery animal.

Choose one of the animals in the picture below. Then answer the questions. The words in the box may help you.

What is it like? _____

What does it look like? _____

What do the body parts look like? _____

What do the body parts do? _____

What can your mystery animal do? _____

How does it move? _____

What is your mystery animal? <u>It is</u> _____.

scary	amazing	big	dangerous	clumsy	little
beautiful	fast	gentle	graceful	huge	strange

> 9.3 Going places

1 Follow the route to the dinosaur museum.

Start on the 'X'. Walk to the library. Draw some books in the library.

Then walk straight ahead to the traffic light. The light says 'Go!'
Colour the light green.

Turn right and walk to the next street, and to the pet shop.
Draw some pets in the shop.

Walk straight ahead past the bus stop.
Turn left to the dinosaur museum. Draw some dinosaurs!

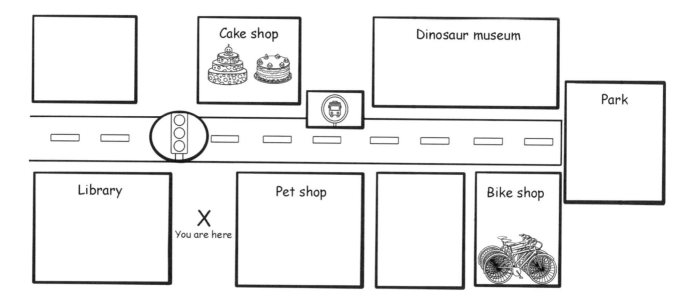

2 Now write instructions to get to a new place.

Start on the 'X'. Walk _____

_____

_____

_____

Draw some swings and a slide in the park!

3 Make a menu.

Make a menu for your café. What food and drinks will you have?

Write them on your menu. You will find some words to help you in the Picture Dictionary in the Learner's Book (page 170).

Menu	
Things to eat	**Things to drink**
_____	_____
_____	_____
_____	_____

4 What would you like to eat?

Write what you say to the waiter. Choose something from your menu!

Waiter:

Would you like something to eat?

Can I _____ _____?

> 9.4 The past, present and future

Focus

1 **Look at the pictures.**
   Then read and complete the poem using the words from the box.

   For each line, choose a verb that begins with same letter as the noun.
   Will you write the verb in the past, present, or future?

   | build   dance   catch   talk   wave   run |

   ### At the zoo

   What will you do when you go to the zoo?

   I will ___build___ with a **b**ee.

   I will play **c**_____ with a **c**ow.

   What are you doing now at the zoo?

   I am _____ with a duck.

   I am _____ with a turtle.

   What did you do yesterday at the zoo?

   I _____ with a rabbit.

   I _____ to a whale.

Practice

2 Complete the questions and match them to the answers.

Then write a different answer, saying what you will do.

a What will you _____do_____ at the zoo? __c__

_____

b What will you _____ at the swimming pool? _____

_____

c What will you _____ at the museum? _____

_____

d What will you _____ at the market? _____

_____

a I will buy some bananas.	c I will wave to the animals.
b I will see my favourite dinosaur.	d I will jump in the water.

Challenge

3 Think of the opposite.

In the future...

a **A:** I will go to the Moon.

B: I ____won't____ go to the Moon. I ____will____ go to Mars.

b **A:** I _____ go to the countryside.

B: I _____.

c **A:** I will live in a cave.

B: _____.

〉 9.5 Opposites

1 Opposites

Look at the words on the left. Do you know their opposites?
Follow the lines to check your answers.

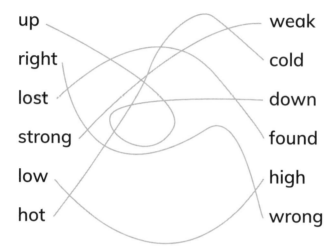

up	weak
right	cold
lost	down
strong	found
low	high
hot	wrong

2 Change the picture.

Read the instructions. Change the picture!

Anna's hair is **short**. Make it **long**.
Anna is **frowning**. Make her **smile**.
It is **day**. Make it **night**.
Anna's boots are **clean**.
Make them **dirty**.

3 Match the -ly words to a picture.

Then complete the sentences.
Sometimes more than one answer is possible.

slowly   quickly   loudly   quietly   happily   sadly   angrily

a She's running for the bus. She's running _____.

b He doesn't want to go to school today. He's walking _____.

c Her team scored a goal. She's shouting _____.

d The other team scored a goal. She's shouting _____.

e The baby's asleep. He's talking _____.

f She won the prize. She's smiling _____.

g She lost the prize. She's sighing _____.

❯ 9.6 City Mouse and Country Mouse

1 Write the words.

Put the letters in the correct order. Write the words on the lines.
Circle the things that you usually find in the city.

a *p o s h* _____

b *f é a c* _____

c *b l i n g i d u* _____

d *w o l* _____

e *e e b s* _____

f *a x i t* _____

Challenge

The story is a **fable**. A fable is a special kind of story where we learn something. What do we learn from this story? Tick (✔) the best answer.

☐ Mice are very silly.

☐ We like the places that we know best.

☐ The city is more scary than the countryside.

2 Cindy or Callie?

Write **Cindy** or **Callie** next to each sentence.

a A cat scared her.

_____

b An owl scared her.

_____

c She liked the city better than the country. _____

d She like the country better than the city. _____

3 Mystery picture

Join the dots. Start from number 1.

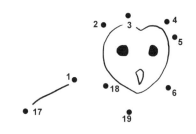

What animal is this?

_____

Does it live in the city or the countryside?

_____

Challenge

Would you like to be the city mouse or the country mouse? Why?

_____

_____

〉 9.7 Check your progress

Listen to your teacher. Tick (✔) the correct pictures.

1 What does the boy want?

a  b  c

2 Where is the boy?

a 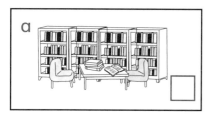 b  c

3 What does the girl want to eat?

a  b  c

4 What does the boy want to drink?

a  b  c

5 Where does the woman want to go?

a  b  c

Read and write.

6 (Circle) the opposite of the word *sit*.

chair   sat   stand

7
Where is the girl?

_____

What is she doing?

_____

_____

8
Where are these girls?

_____

What are they doing?

_____

_____

Reflection

Talk with a partner

What did you enjoy doing in this unit?

☐ role-playing shopping

☐ role-playing ordering food in a café

☐ using describing words, such as *quickly*

☐ practising giving and following directions

☐ using opposite words

☐ reading and discussing a story about the differences in the city and the countryside

What would you like more help with?

☐ role-playing shopping

☐ role-playing ordering food in a café

☐ using describing words, such as *quickly*

☐ practising giving and following directions

☐ using opposite words

☐ reading and discussing a story about the differences in the city and the countryside